D1397494

Seeing

See for Yourself

Seeing

Brenda Walpole
Photographs by Barrie Watts

RSVP

RAINTREE
STECK-VAUGHN
PUBLISHERS
The Steck-Vaughn Company

Austin, Texas

Published by Raintree Steck-Vaughn Publishers, an imprint of Steck-Vaughn Company

Editor: Kathy DeVico
Project Manager: Amy Atkinson
Electronic Production: Scott Melcer

All photographs by Barrie Watts except for:
p. 13 Alan Becker/Image Bank; p. 15 Mark Richards/PhotoEdit; p. 16 Laurie Campbell/NHPA; p. 19 A.N.T./NHPA; p. 20 Patrick Fagot/NHPA; p. 21 Jean-Louis Le Moigne/NHPA; p. 25 Manfred Kage/Science Photo Library.

Library of Congress Cataloging-in-Publication Data
Walpole, Brenda.
    Seeing / Brenda Walpole; photographs by Barrie Watts.
        p.   cm. — (See for yourself)
    Includes index.
    Summary: Introduces the concept of seeing and suggests activities which reinforce the understanding of this sense.
    ISBN 0-8172-4218-X
    1. Vision — Juvenile literature. [1. Vision. 2. Senses and sensation.] I. Watts, Barrie, ill. II. Title. III. Series.
    QP475.7.W35   1997
    612.8'4 — dc20   96-11076
                                          CIP
                                          AC

Printed and bound in the United States
1 2 3 4 5 6 7 8 9 0 LB 99 98 97 96

Contents

What Our Eyes Can See

What can you see if you look out of the window?
You might see something moving.
Or you might see something so large that you can only see a part of it.
What is the smallest thing that you can see?

Your eyes tell you more about the world than any of your other senses. Your eyes can see color and movement. They help you figure out how big things are and how far away they are.

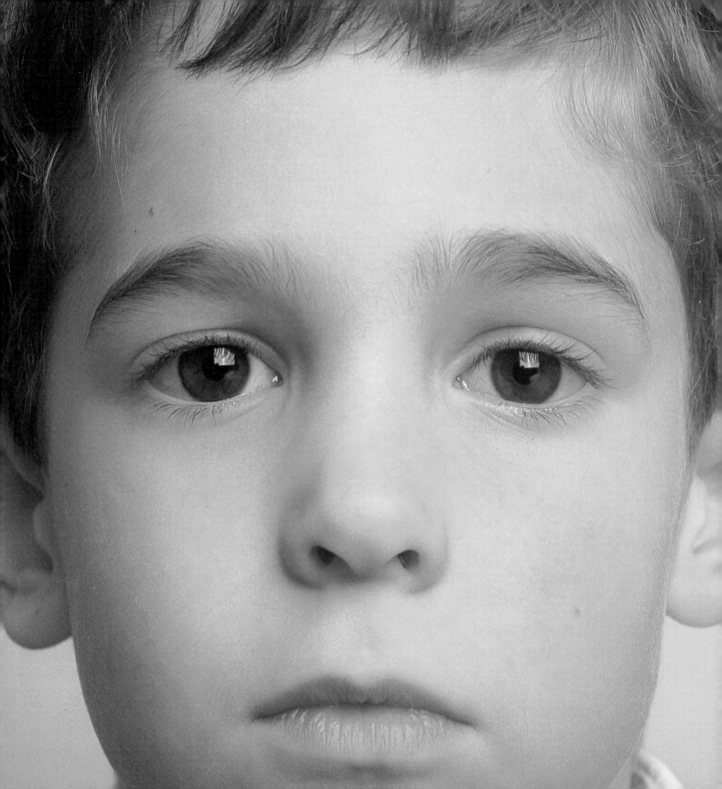

Why We Need Light

When it is dark, we cannot see very well.
Our eyes need light to see.

Close your eyes for a moment.
If you couldn't see, you would have to rely on your
other senses: smell, taste, touch, and hearing.

Imagine that you couldn't use
your eyes. Make up a story
about going on a shopping trip.
How could you use your other
senses to help you? When would
each sense be most useful?

When we are tired, or when we
go to sleep, we close our eyes.
Can you think of any other times
when people close their eyes?

Protecting Our Eyes

When you blink, tears wash over
the fronts of your eyes.
If a speck of dust gets into your
eye, your eye starts to water
because it is making extra tears
to wash the dust out.
What other things
make your eyes water?

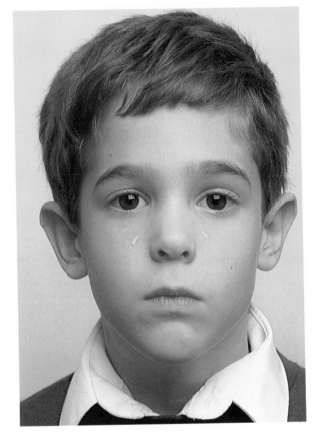

Very bright light can damage
your sight. That's why it is very
dangerous to look directly at the
sun or at a bright lamp. How do
people protect their eyes on very
sunny days?

Find out how your eyes adjust to
light. Switch on a table lamp, and place a mirror near it.
Use the mirror to look at the small black circles, called pupils,
that are in the middle of your eyes. Now turn off the lamp.
Wait for about 30 seconds, and look into the mirror again.
What has happened to your pupils?
How do you think they help protect your eyes?

10

Seeing Colors

We usually say that sunlight is white.
But did you know that sunlight is really made up
of lots of different colors?

Look at the big picture.
How many different colors can you see in the rainbow?
Sometimes, after a storm, the sun shines
when it is still raining. As sunlight
passes through the raindrops, we see
all of these colors.

You can make these different
colors turn back into one color.
Cut out a circle of white cardboard,
and color in the main rainbow
colors in this order: red,
orange, yellow, green, blue,
and purple. Sharpen a
pencil, and carefully push
it through the middle of the
cardboard circle. Spin the
circle like a top. What color
do you see as it spins?

Colorful Warnings

Colors can sometimes act as warnings.

A red traffic light means stop right away. Red is a color that usually means danger. Fire engines, hot water faucets, and signs all have red markings.

Police officers and firefighters sometimes wear brightly colored safety jackets. Parts of these jackets are made of reflective material that can be seen in the dark. Cyclists often wear safety belts and armbands made of shiny material so that they can be seen easily.

Can you find the signs for a school, roadworks, or a one-way street near your home? Draw some of the other signs that you see. What shapes are they? Which colors are used most often?

Different Eyes

Some animals have much better eyesight than we do.
Owls hunt for small animals, such as mice and voles.
To find their prey, owls need excellent eyesight.
They have two large eyes at the front of their head so
they can judge distance well. Owls can see well,
even when it is dark outside.

A rabbit has one eye
on each side of its
head. It can see well
to the sides and
behind. A rabbit can
spot any enemies
that may be trying to
sneak up on it.

Moles have very poor eyesight.
They live underground where there is no light.
Can you guess how they find their way around?

How Animals Use Colors

Many birds use their colorful feathers to attract attention.

During the mating season, a male peacock opens up his huge tail when females pass by. He waves it to show off his beautiful feathers. The peacock that has the best tail will be the one that is noticed by the females.

This male Siamese fighting fish uses its brightly colored fins to attract females. The males also use their fins to warn off other males. They spread their fins out to make themselves look bigger and more dangerous.

Some animals use their colors as a warning. This frog is poisonous. The poison can kill other animals that try to eat the frog. Its bright color warns other animals to stay away.

Hidden Life

Can you see the stick insect in the big photograph?
It is almost impossible to find a stick insect on a branch,
because its body and its colors are so much like the trees
it lives in. If stick insects stay still, they can hide for hours.

Many animals disguise themselves with colors and patterns.
They blend in with their surroundings and can stay hidden
from enemies.

A tiger has stripes
that blend in with
tall grass and
undergrowth.
It can stalk its
prey without
being seen. It can
also stay hidden
until it is ready
to pounce.

Bird-watchers need to get close to wild birds without disturbing
them. Draw some outfits that they could wear to blend in with the
surroundings in woods, a rocky place, or a snowy landscape.

20

Improving Our Eyesight

Not everyone has perfect eyesight. Many of us need glasses to help us see clearly.

Some people are nearsighted. Without glasses, they have to hold a book very close to their eyes to read it. Other people are farsighted. They need to hold a book at arm's length.

A pair of glasses has lenses that help our eyes focus properly and see clearly. Contact lenses do the same thing, but they are small enough to fit onto each eye.

Borrow a pair of glasses (but don't forget to ask first), and hold them over this page. How do the lenses change the shapes and sizes of the letters? Try different pairs of glasses, and see what happens.

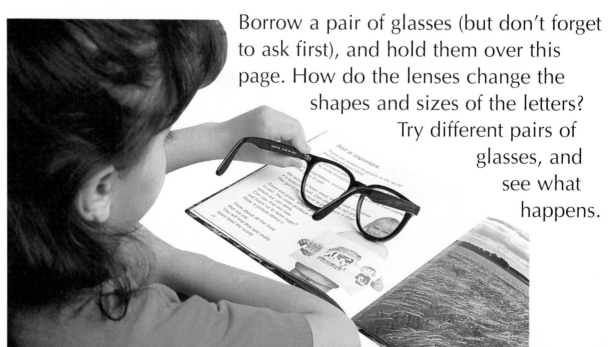

Soil

See for yourself
what soil is made of, how
to make compost and why
earthworms are good for the soil.

See for yourself

Stunning colour photographs are the starting point
for simple scientific investigations based on
the natural world, with bold headings
for very young children and more
detailed information for
slightly older readers.

Making Things Look Bigger

A hand lens contains a strong lens that helps us to see small things. Through a hand lens, you can see the details on a stamp or look closely at a small insect.

Can you see how the hand lens makes the writing appear larger in the picture below?
Try drawing this "Q" as big as it is here. Now look at it through a hand lens, and draw it again. How much bigger is it?

Microscopes have several lenses inside of them. They can make things seem as much as one thousand times larger. Through a microscope, we can look closely at tiny animals or even at the hairs on a fly's leg.

The big picture was taken through a microscope. What do you think it is?

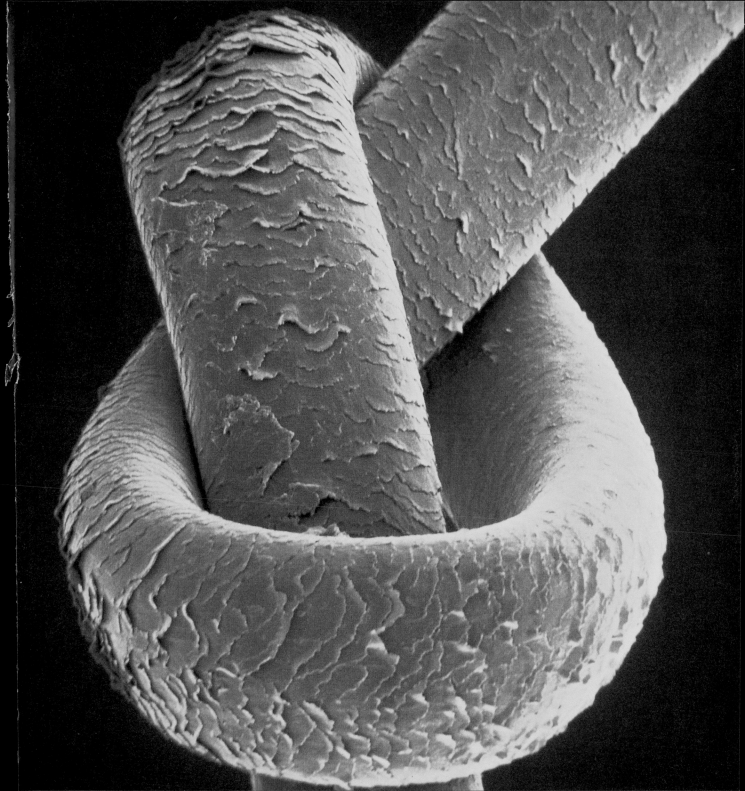

Illusions

Your eyes see what is in front of them, but it is your brain that decides what you are seeing. If what you see is not all there or not quite as you expected, your brain fills in the gaps to make it seem right. You end up seeing what you expect to be there. We call pictures like these illusions.

Look at the big picture. Is it a picture of a vase or of two people's faces?

Which one of these lines is longer?
Guess first, and then measure both of them.

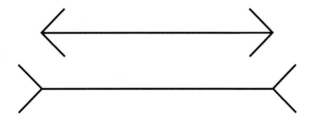

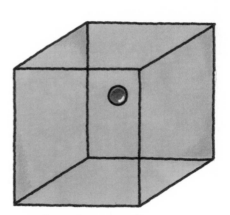

Is the dot at the front or at the back of the cube?

Are the stairs on the floor or on the ceiling in this picture?

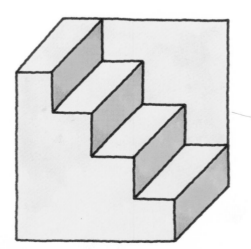

More Things to Do

1. A pencil test
We need two eyes to judge distances properly.
Hold two pencils, pointing them toward each
other. Close one eye, and try to bring the
pencils together so that their points touch.
Can you do it the first time?

2. Make your own mini-magnifier.
Cut a small, round hole in a piece of cardboard.
Stick a piece of clear tape across the hole. Use
a straw to put a round drop of water on top of
the tape. Now try looking through the droplet
at the words in a book or a newspaper. Do the
words appear larger through the droplet?

3. Fool yourself!
Find a small cardboard tube, or roll up a piece
of paper into a tube. Keep both eyes open, and
look through the tube with your right eye. At the
same time, hold your left hand up next to the
tube, with your palm toward you. You should see
that there seems to be a hole in your left hand!

Answer for page 24:
The picture on page 25 is of a human hair that
has been tied in a knot. It is shown three
hundred times larger than its normal size.

Index

This index will help you find some
of the important words in this book.

Notes for Parents and Teachers

These notes will give you some additional information about the senses and suggest some more activities you might like to try with the children.

Pages 6–9

Eighty percent of the brain's input is thought to come from sight. Inside the eye, there are two types of light-sensitive cells, called cones and rods. They are found in the outermost layer of the retina, and are connected to sensory nerves. Cones are sensitive to colored light. Humans have three types of cones. Each one is most sensitive to either the red, blue, or green wavelength of light. The colors we perceive are combinations of these wavelengths. Rods are extremely sensitive to light, but cannot detect color. They enable us to see in dim light, but only in black, white, and shades of gray.

Pages 10–11

The iris contains muscles that alter the size of the pupil, enabling the pupil to dilate in dim light and contract in bright light. Pupil diameter can vary from 1–6 mm.

Eye color is inherited. Generally, brown is dominant to blue, but a brown-eyed parent can have a blue-eyed child. The children could make a survey of eye color in their class to discover which color occurs most frequently. They might also try a similar survey in their immediate family, to see how eye color has been passed on.

Pages 12–13

There are three main bands of color in the spectrum—red, green, and blue. These are called the primary colors of light. When the red wavelength of light reflects off a surface, we see the color red. The remaining wavelengths in the spectrum are absorbed by that surface. If all the colors in the spectrum are reflected by a surface, we see white. If all the colors in the spectrum are absorbed by a surface, there is an absence of color—black.

The primary colors of paint are red, yellow, and blue. By mixing different combinations of these colors, we can create other colors. Can the children create orange, green, and purple using only the three primary colors?

Pages 20–21

Color and pattern are important in camouflage. The snowshoe hare, which lives in the Arctic, has white fur during the winter. This helps to camouflage it against the snow. In the spring, as the snow melts, the hare grows a brown coat to blend in with its changing surroundings.

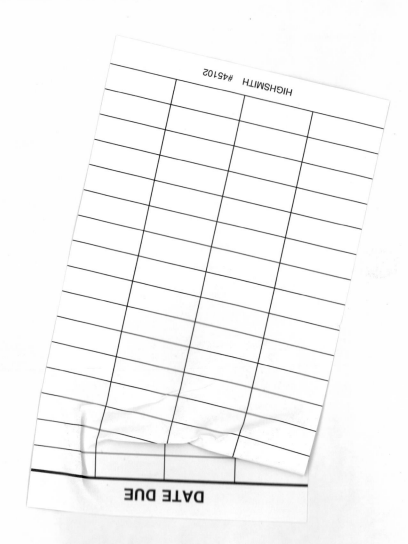

HIGHSMITH #45102

DATE DUE